A COMPANION JOURNAL FOR
"THE AUTHOR'S ACCOUNTABILITY PLANNER"

WRITING PROMPTS TO KEEP YOU
ACCOUNTABLE

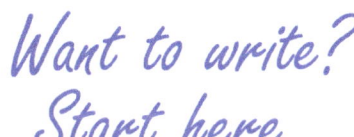

Want to write?
Start here...

2025

DR. JENIFER PAQUETTE

Accomplishing
Innovation Press

4 Horsemen
Publications, Inc.

Accomplishing
Innovation Press

Published By: Accomplishing Innovation Press an imprint of 4 Horsemen Publications, Inc.

Accomplishing Innovation Press
℅ 4 Horsemen Publications, Inc.
PO Box 419
Sylva, NC 28779
4horsemenpublications.com
info@4horsemenpublications.com

Cover & Typesetting by Valerie Willis
Illustrations from © Evgenii Naumov | Dreamstime.com
Stock photos taken from Shutterstock.com and Dreamstime.com

Library of Congress Control Number: 2024950654

Paperback ISBN-13: 979-8-8232-0753-9
eBook ISBN-13: 979-8-8232-0754-6

DEDICATION

To the Writing Hours Crew, who keep me accountable

How to Use This Book

Welcome, fellow writer! This book is designed to accompany the 4HP *Author's Accountability Planner* for 2025, so you'll find that the weekly themes mirror those in that book (check it out if you don't know what that is!). Don't worry if you don't have that book, though. These writing prompts can be used at any time, regardless of whether you are also keeping yourself accountable with the planner.

Essentially, there are two ways to use this book:

1. Follow along with each weekly theme that corresponds to the week of the year. In the Accountability Planner for 2025, January is the "Getting Started" month, so you'll find weekly themes of brainstorming (you'll see my cheesy pun in a moment!), narrowing your focus, goal setting, avoiding shiny objects, and starting a writing habit. The January writing prompts correlate with those concepts, sometimes directly and sometimes indirectly. You can work your way through this book chronologically, spending each week working on a new story or scene to keep your writing muscles primed.

2. You can completely disregard the chronological order, flip through until a prompt catches your fancy, and write that instead. You don't have to follow the order or even all of the instructions. Let the writing take you where it needs to go. These are designed to be writing exercises, practice, so use them that way. They don't have to be completed. They don't have to go any-where. And if you are inspired to keep going, don't stop. Let the words flow now that you have been prompted.

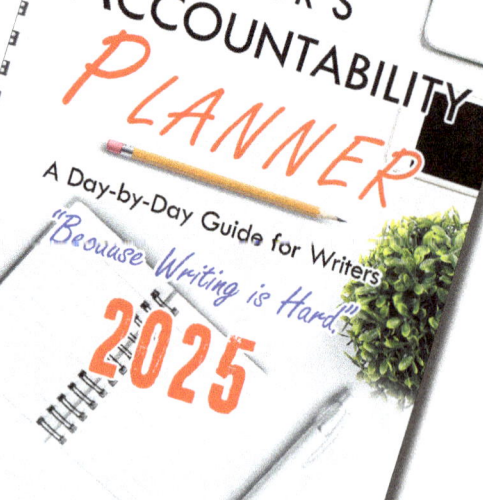

A quick note about layout:

For those of you who like to see what's coming: here's a brief overview of the weekly themes. Each month has five to six prompts, depending on the number of weeks. Every three months, there is a Quarterly Break with some fun prompts, available to use at your leisure.

JANUARY - GETTING STARTED
Week 1: Brainstorming
Week 2: Narrowing Your Focus
Week 3: Goal Setting
Week 4: Avoiding Shiny Objects
Week 5: Starting a Writing Habit

FEBRUARY - PLOT
Week 1: Pacing
Week 2: Story Beats
Week 3: Filling Plot Holes
Week 4: Character vs World Driven
Week 5: An Original or Formula Beats

MARCH - CHARACTER
Week 1: Character Inspiration
Week 2: Character Goals
Week 3: Character Motivation
Week 4: Character Conflict
Week 5: Dialogue
Week 6: Character Growth

APRIL - SETTING & WORLDBUILDING
Week 1: Creating Your World
Week 2: Tracking Your World
Week 3: Time Period
Week 4: Geographic Space
Week 5: The Real World

MAY - AUTHOR MOTIVATION
Wcck 1: Staking Motivated
Week 2: Keep the Carrot Relevant
Week 3: Fight Imposter Syndrome
Week 4: Reward Systems
Week 5: Validation

JUNE- SHAMELESS SELF PROMOTION
Week 1: Branding
Week 2: Website & Newsletter
Week 3: Social Media
Week 4: Conventions & Bookstores
Week 5: Reviews

JULY - LEARNING THE CRAFT
Week 1: Learn the Tools of the Craft
Week 2: Grammar
Week 3: Punctuation
Week 4: Writer Resources
Week 5: Recognize Your Strengths

AUGUST - REVISIONS AND EDITING
Week 1: Re-read Your Work
Week 2: Developmental Editing
Week 3: Revision
Week 4: Editing
Week 5: Let It Go

SEPTEMBER - RESEARCH
Week 1: Character Focus
Week 2: Plot Focus
Week 3: World Focus
Week 4: Rabbit Holes
Week 5: Integrating Fact into Fiction

OCTOBER - GENRE
Week 1: Genre Expectations
Week 2: Point-of-View
Week 3: Tense
Week 4: Mood
Week 5: Step Outside the Box

NOVEMBER - THE WRITING HABIT
Week 1: Staying Motivated
Week 2: Tracking Your Progress
Week 3: Accountability Buddies
Week 4: Revel in Your Accomplishments
Week 5: Finish Line

DECEMBER - SELF-CARE
Week 1: Take a break
Week 2: Change of Scenery
Week 3: Plan with Other Authors
Week 4: Treat Yourself
Week 5: Resources

ACCOUNTABILITY

AUTHOR BIO

WHO ARE YOU ANYWAY?

Dr. Jenifer Paquette has been editing everything from creative fiction to technical dissertations for over twenty years. As Lead Editor for 4 Horsemen Publications, she loves helping authors polish their prose to a lustrous sheen. She spent decades teaching English in higher education exploring the history of the English language as well as the intricacies of grammar rules (#OxfordComma). When she isn't debating what part of the punctuation gets italics when foreign and English words mix inside dialogue, Dr. Paquette spends her time writing fantasy and paranormal romance novels as JM Paquette. When she isn't writing, she can be found dissecting grammar, defending fantasy, discussing Tolkien, editing books, guest co-hosting the podcast *Drinking with Authors,* reading books with happy endings, and watching Russian dragon shifter movies.

WRITE YOUR BIO HERE

_____

_____

_____

_____

_____

_____

_____

_____

_____

_____

_____

_____

_____

ACCOUNTABILITY

DOODLE TIME!

JANUARY

> "It was a dark and stormy night."
> Write a short scene involving the weather.

JANUARY

JANUARY

JANUARY

WEEK 2

Write a scene that starts with the big picture, then slowly narrows down to one focal point.

JANUARY

JANUARY

JANUARY

JANUARY

WEEK 3

66

Write a story that uses the idea of a goal—someone scores,
a deadline is attained or missed, etc.

99

JANUARY

JANUARY

JANUARY

WEEK 4

Write a story about a character who
is distracted.

_____

_____

_____

_____

_____

_____

_____

_____

_____

_____

_____

_____

_____

_____

JANUARY

_____

_____

_____

_____

_____

_____

_____

_____

_____

_____

_____

_____

_____

JANUARY

JANUARY

> Write the first paragraph of a story. Then, write a different first paragraph for the same story. Repeat. Try to create five different possible beginnings for the same story concept.

JANUARY

JANUARY

JANUARY

FEBRUARY

" Write a scene about a character who is pacing. Why are they walking back and forth? What troubles them? Who are they waiting for? "

FEBRUARY

FEBRUARY

FEBRUARY

FEBRUARY

> Write a story that includes music, specifically the steady
> beat of an instrument.

_____

_____

_____

_____

_____

_____

_____

_____

_____

_____

_____

_____

_____

_____

_____

FEBRUARY

FEBRUARY

FEBRUARY

FEBRUARY

> Write a scene about a character who is either digging or filling in a hole.

FEBRUARY

FEBRUARY

FEBRUARY

> Write a conversation where world events have driven your
> character to laughter or tears (or both).

FEBRUARY

FEBRUARY

FEBRUARY

> Write a scene where the setting is directly fighting against
> a character (man vs volcano, sailor vs riptide, etc.).

_____

_____

_____

_____

_____

_____

_____

_____

_____

_____

_____

_____

_____

_____

_____

FEBRUARY

FEBRUARY

WEEK 1

> Write a speech your main character might give about their inspiration. What drives them?

_____

_____

_____

_____

_____

_____

_____

_____

_____

_____

_____

_____

_____

_____

_____

MARCH

MARCH

MARCH

"
Describe a character's favorite memory the way they would share it with a friend or loved one. How would they tell the story?
"

MARCH

MARCH

MARCH

MARCH

> Write a scene where a character reveals a surprising
> motivation for their current actions. Surprise the reader
> (and yourself) with a different reason than you
> first anticipated.

MARCH

MARCH

MARCH

> Write a fight scene. Choose your time period, setting, characters, and weapons, and describe the action for readers.

MARCH

MARCH

MARCH

> Write a scene where two of your characters from completely different worlds and stories interact. What do they say to one another?

MARCH

MARCH

WEEK 6

> Jot down some fun top fives for the world of your story:
> songs everyone knows, news stories everyone has heard
> about, and most popular gifts to give a loved one on
> their birthday.

MARCH

MARCH

QUARTERLY BREAK

HAVE SOME FUN!

COFFEE VS TEA. DISCUSS.

_____

_____

_____

WHAT IS YOUR GO-TO WRITING DRINK? WHY?

_____

_____

_____

RECORD THE DETAILS OF YOUR LAST WRITING SESSION. WHEN WAS IT?

_____

_____

_____

WHERE WERE YOU?

_____

_____

_____

ACCOUNTABILITY

WHAT DID YOU WORK ON? HOW DID IT GO?

_____

_____

_____

_____

HOW DID IT FEEL?

_____

_____

_____

_____

WRITE A SYNOPSIS OF THE EXPERIENCE.

_____

_____

_____

_____

WHAT IS YOUR FAVORITE THING TO LISTEN TO WHILE WRITING?

_____

_____

_____

_____

WRITE ABOUT THE AMBIENCE YOU ENJOY WHILE WRITING.

_____

_____

_____

_____

ACCOUNTABILITY

APRIL

"
Write a creation story, a myth about how the world came
to be. How did it start? Then, think about who would be
telling this story, and who would be listening/reading it.
"

APRIL

WEEK 2

> Write a story that involves the passing of time or the
> changing of seasons.

APRIL

APRIL

> Imagine a modern device were to somehow appear in the past. Write a scene about the people of the past and their reaction to this advanced contraption. (What would the 16th century make of a modern can opener?)

_____

_____

_____

_____

_____

_____

_____

_____

_____

_____

_____

_____

_____

_____

_____

APRIL

APRIL

APRIL

> Write a story that takes place somewhere that you
> have never been, somewhere far away from your lived
> experience.

APRIL

APRIL

APRIL

> Write a scene about a behavior or tradition seems normal
> to one character yet scandalizes the other.

APRIL

MAY

> Write a scene about an author who is sucked into their current work in progress. What happens?

MAY

MAY

MAY

MAY

"
Write an outline for a story with the top-selling tropes in your genre right now. If it's mafia romance, start with a kidnapping. If it's thriller, start with the body in a ditch. See if you can find some story beats that would fit if you ever do decide to write to market.
"

MAY

MAY

MAY

> Write a story about an imposter. Who are they really?
> What are they doing in this place they don't belong?

MAY

MAY

MAY

> Write a conversation between two people who have just won a lottery. This can be a good thing (Megamillions!) or not (think Shirley Jackson's "The Lottery" or the 2005 film "The Island." Haven't read or seen it? You've got some homework!).

MAY

MAY

MAY

MAY

MAY

> Write a story about a world that has a different concept of validation—what are the markers of success?

MAY

_____

_____

_____

_____

_____

_____

_____

_____

_____

_____

_____

_____

_____

_____

_____

MAY

MAY

JUNE

> Write a story that involves branding—in whatever way works for your genre and writing style. Does someone develop their marketing brand, or does someone get jabbed with a hot iron rod?

JUNE

JUNE

JUNE

> Write a story about someone receiving a chain letter (Pass this on to ten people and good fortune will find you!). The twist: this one is real.

_____

_____

_____

_____

_____

_____

_____

_____

_____

_____

_____

_____

_____

_____

> Write a text message conversation between two main characters. What do they talk about? (And does one use proper punctuation? Grin.) Do some research to see current standards on formatting text messages in fiction.

JUNE

JUNE

JUNE

JUNE

> Write a scene that takes place in a bookstore. You know you have an idea for this one.

JUNE

JUNE

> " Write a performance review or evaluation of how well a character is doing their "job" in the story—how did the person do? What parts are they performing well? What aspects need work? (Is your villain getting the job done?) "

JUNE

JUNE

QUARTERLY BREAK

HAVE SOME FUN!

CATS VS DOGS. DISCUSS.

_____

_____

_____

_____

_____

_____

_____

REWRITE A SCENE YOU HAVE ALREADY WRITTEN FROM THE PERSPECTIVE OF A PET WHO ALSO WITNESSES THE EVENTS.

_____

_____

_____

_____

_____

_____

_____

ACCOUNTABILITY

WHAT DOES YOUR PET DO ALL DAY WHEN YOU AREN'T HOME?

_____
_____
_____
_____
_____
_____
_____
_____

WRITE A STORY ABOUT A CHARACTER'S FIRST INTERACTION WITH A NON-HUMAN.

_____
_____
_____
_____
_____
_____
_____
_____
_____

ACCOUNTABILITY

JULY

> Write a story about a character who learns a new trade or skill. Choose something you already know about so this doesn't turn into a rabbit hole of research. Focus on the story of how someone learns a new thing instead of the minutiae of the hobby.

JULY

JULY

JULY

WEEK 2

JULY

JULY

WEEK 3

> Write a scene involving the printing process. Characters can lay out books for printing the old-fashioned way or can send them digitally or can discuss the logistics of getting their books to a certain location on time (like ordering enough for a convention appearance, perhaps!).

JULY

JULY

> Write a story that focuses on a book as the central item of importance. It could be a book everyone is after, a book someone is writing, a book someone is hiding, whatever!

JULY

JULY

JULY

"Write a story about a character who is super strong in some way.

_____

_____

_____

_____

_____

_____

_____

_____

_____

_____

_____

_____

_____

_____

_____

_____

_____

_____

_____

JULY

JULY

AUGUST

> Write a story about a character who discovers an old
> message (letter/email/note/whatever). What does it say?
> Who was it meant for? What does the character do with it?

_____

_____

_____

_____

_____

_____

_____

_____

_____

_____

_____

_____

_____

AUGUST

WEEK 2

> Write a scene about a character who has undergone a
> major change and is sharing the news with an old friend.

AUGUST

> "Write a scene where a couple breaks up. Have them mention the reasons why the relationship is over. Now, go back and rewrite that scene, but have them say different things so that they don't break up."

WEEK 4

> Write a story that centers on a sharp edge—
> a knife, a sword, a thin piece of paper.

AUGUST

WEEK 5

> Write a story about letting go. Who is letting go of what and why?

AUGUST

SEPTEMBER

WEEK 1

SEPTEMBER

SEPTEMBER

SEPTEMBER

September

> Write a scene where truth and reality come into conflict.
> What does truth mean in this story? What is reality?

SEPTEMBER

_____

_____

_____

_____

_____

_____

_____

_____

_____

_____

_____

_____

_____

SEPTEMBER

SEPTEMBER

SEPTEMBER

> Write a story about an important historical event that coincides with an important personal event for one of your characters.

_____

_____

_____

_____

_____

_____

_____

_____

_____

_____

_____

_____

_____

_____

_____

SEPTEMBER

SEPTEMBER

SEPTEMBER

SEPTEMBER

September

" Write a story about rabbits. They can go to war, like
in "Watership Down," or they can be fluffy friendly
bunnies like Peter Rabbit. Write the genre you love. But
about bunnies. "

SEPTEMBER

September

> Write a story about an event that has been greatly exaggerated in the telling. What really happened? What do people think happened?

_____

_____

_____

_____

_____

_____

_____

_____

_____

_____

_____

_____

_____

_____

_____

_____

SEPTEMBER

SEPTEMBER

QUARTERLY BREAK

HAVE SOME FUN!

INSIDE VS OUTSIDE. DISCUSS.

_____

_____

_____

_____

_____

_____

WRITE A DISCUSSION BETWEEN TWO CHARACTERS WHERE ONE PREFERS TO BE INDOORS AND THE OTHER WANTS TO GO OUTSIDE.

_____

_____

_____

_____

_____

ACCOUNTABILITY

REVISIT A SCENE OR STORY YOU HAVE ALREADY WRITTEN AND THINK ABOUT THE SETTING. WHERE DOES IT TAKE PLACE AND HOW DOES THE SETTING INFLUENCE THE STORY?

_____

_____

_____

_____

_____

_____

_____

TAKE A POPULAR STORY OR SCENE YOU KNOW AND REWRITE IT SO IT TAKES PLACE IN A COMPLETELY DIFFERENT PLACE—PUT ROSE AND JACK AT THE ZOO INSTEAD OF THE SINKING _TITANIC_, MOVE INDIANA JONES AND HIS FATHER TO A SANDY BEACH INSTEAD OF A LOST TEMPLE HIDING THE HOLY GRAIL, ETC. HOW WOULD THE EVENTS SHIFT IN THAT NEW PLACE?

_____

_____

_____

_____

_____

_____

_____

A C C O U N T A B I L I T Y

OCTOBER

> Write a scene about broken expectations.

OCTOBER

OCTOBER

OCTOBER

OCTOBER

OCTOBER

"
Write a story about falling in love using 1st person point of view. Now, rewrite it from the other person's point of view. If you like this story, rewrite it in 3rd person to get an outside view. Looking for a challenge? Rewrite it in 2nd person, telling the reader what "you" are doing.
"

OCTOBER

OCTOBER

OCTOBER

OCTOBER

> Write an action scene in present tense. Now, rewrite that scene in past tense. Which do you prefer?

OCTOBER

_____

_____

_____

_____

_____

_____

_____

_____

_____

_____

_____

_____

_____

_____

_____

OCTOBER

OCTOBER

> Pick a number between 1 and 3. Now, write a scene with a
> specific mood in mind.
> (1: Comical. 2: Dramatic. 3: Tragic.)

WEEK 5

Write a story featuring a box. What is the box holding?
What does it symbolize? Why should readers care
about this box?

OCTOBER

OCTOBER

_____

_____

_____

_____

_____

_____

_____

_____

_____

_____

_____

_____

_____

_____

_____

_____

OCTOBER

NOVEMBER

WEEK 1

"
Write a story about racing. It can involve any form of racing (cars, bikes, boats, legs, wings, fingers, whatever!).
"

NOVEMBER

NOVEMBER

NOVEMBER

NOVEMBER

WEEK 2

Write a story about a terrible weather event that threatens the lives of your characters.

_____

_____

_____

_____

_____

_____

_____

_____

_____

_____

_____

_____

_____

_____

_____

NOVEMBER

NOVEMBER

WEEK 3

> Write a story about four lifelong friends who have gotten together in a remote cabin for a long-awaited reunion.

_____

_____

_____

_____

_____

_____

_____

_____

_____

_____

_____

_____

_____

_____

_____

_____

_____

NOVEMBER

NOVEMBER

WEEK 4

> Write a story about winning an award or getting recognition of some kind.

NOVEMBER

NOVEMBER

NOVEMBER

NOVEMBER

WEEK 5

> Write a scene about a deadline that two characters are fighing to meet first.

NOVEMBER

NOVEMBER

DECEMBER

WEEK 1

DECEMBER

DECEMBER

DECEMBER

DECEMBER

> Write a story in which the scenery is practically a character by itself.

DECEMBER

"
Write a scene of an awkward get together. Who is there?
Why is it weird?
"

_____

_____

_____

_____

_____

_____

_____

_____

_____

_____

_____

_____

_____

_____

_____

DECEMBER

_____

_____

_____

_____

_____

_____

_____

_____

_____

_____

_____

_____

_____

_____

_____

DECEMBER

December

"Write a scene of a character convincing themselves they deserve a treat. What do they deserve and why? (Are they buying a new purse, or are they letting the voices convince them to murder that guy?)"

_____

_____

_____

_____

_____

_____

_____

_____

_____

_____

_____

_____

_____

_____

_____

_____

_____

_____

_____

_____

_____

_____

_____

_____

_____

_____

_____

_____

_____

_____

DECEMBER

DECEMBER

> Write a story about the end of something. Could be the
> end of the year, the end of a project, the end of a career—
> just focus on something being over.

_____

_____

_____

_____

_____

_____

_____

_____

_____

_____

_____

_____

December

DECEMBER

DECEMBER

QUARTERLY BREAK

HAVE SOME FUN!

ENDINGS VS BEGINNINGS. DISCUSS.

_____

_____

_____

_____

_____

_____

_____

THINK ABOUT WHERE YOU WERE AT THE START OF THIS YEAR. HOW DO YOU FEEL ABOUT YOUR JOURNEY THESE PAST MONTHS?

_____

_____

_____

_____

_____

_____

_____

ACCOUNTABILITY

ACCOUNTABILITY

WHAT ADVICE WOULD YOU GIVE YOUR FORMER SELF NOW THAT ANOTHER YEAR HAS PASSED?

_____

_____

_____

_____

_____

_____

_____

_____

WHAT WERE SOME OF THE BEST THINGS ABOUT THIS YEAR? RECORD THEM NOW!

_____

_____

_____

_____

_____

_____

_____

_____

DOODLE TIME!